EAST OF THE SUN

SENIOR AUTHOR

JACK BOOTH

DAVID BOOTH

WILLA PAULI & JO PHENIX

IMPRESSIONS

HOLT, RINEHART AND WINSTON OF CANADA, LIMITED

1989 Printing

Senior Editor: Wendy Cochran
Developmental Editor: Deborah Gordon Lewi
Production Editor: Jocelyn Van Huyse
Design: Wycliffe Smith
Art Direction: Holly Fisher
Cover Illustrator: Heather Cooper

ISBN 0-03-926808-X

Canadian Cataloguing in Publication Data

Main entry under title:
East of the Sun

(Impressions)
For use in schools.
ISBN 0-03-926808-X

1. Readers (Primary).   2. Readers – 1950 –
I. Booth, Jack, 1946 –   II. Series.

PE1119.H69   428.6   C83-098250-7

Illustrations

Sylvie Daigneault: pp. 6-7, 70-80; *Jock MacRae:* pp. 8, 9, 231; *Greg Duffell* and *Mary Young:* pp. 10-16; *Vladyana Krykorka:* pp. 21, 42, 52-53, 82-86, 242; *I. Aliki:* pp. 22-31; *M.B. Goffstein:* pp. 33-35; *Robert Kraus:* pp. 38-41; *Joanne Fitzgerald:* pp. 32, 98-99, 156-157, 176-182; *Michele Nidenoff:* pp. 36, 37; *San Murata:* pp. 43-51; *Barbara Klunder:* pp. 54-57, 158-166; *Marie-Louise Cussack:* pp. 17-20; *Ian Leventhal:* pp. 58-62; *Tina Seemann:* p. 63; *Krystna De Duleba:* pp. 64-69; *Brenda Clark:* pp. 81, 94-95, 100; *Rose Zgodzinski:* p. 87; *Bryon Barton:* pp. 88-93; *Magda Markowski:* pp. 96-97, 253-256; *James Marshall:* pp. 101-104; *Vesna Krystanovich:* pp. 105, 154-155, 183; *Jack Kent:* pp. 106-119; *Pat Gagnon:* pp. 120-121; *Rosemary Wells:* pp. 122-135; *Deborah Robison:* pp. 136-145; *Glen Priestly:* pp. 146-153; *Philippe Beha:* pp. 167-175; *Arnold Lobel:* pp. 184-189, 206-219, 232-241; *Judith Kern:* pp. 190-199; *Helen Marioncu:* pp. 200-201; *Joe Weissmann:* pp. 202, 203; *Lisa Smith:* p. 205; *Frank Hammond:* pp. 220-225; *Ezra Jack Keats:* pp. 226-230; *Ossie Murray:* pp. 243-249; *Caroline Price:* pp. 250-252.

The authors and publishers gratefully acknowledge the consultants listed below for their contribution to the development of this program:

Isobel Bryan   *Primary Consultant   Ottawa Board of Education*
Ethel Buchanan   *Language Arts Consultant   Winnipeg, Manitoba*
Heather Hayes   *Elementary Curriculum Consultant   City of Halifax Board of Education*
Gary Heck   *Curriculum Co-ordinator, Humanities   Lethbridge School District No. 51*
Ina Mary Rutherford   *Supervisor of Reading and Primary Instruction   Bruce County Board of Education*
Janice M. Sarkissian   *Supervisor of Instruction (Primary and Pre-School)   Greater Victoria School District*
Lynn Taylor   *Language Arts Consultant   Saskatoon Catholic School Board*

Printed in the United States of America   0123 063 7654

Acknowledgements

The Animals' Walk: By Dolores Hind. Reprinted by permission of DOLORES HIND LTD. "Hindsite," R.R. #4, Shelburne, Ont., L0N 1S0. *I Want a Small Piece of String*: Reprinted by permission of Four Winds Press, a division of Scholastic Inc. from ARM & ARM by Remy Charlip. Copyright © 1969 by Remy Charlip. *Fresh Cider and Pie*: By Franz Brandenberg, illustrations by Aliki Brandenberg. Reprinted with permission of Macmillan Publishing Co., Inc. from FRESH CIDER AND PIE by Franz Brandenberg, illustrated by Aliki Brandenberg. Copyright © 1973 by Franz Brandenberg. Copyright © 1973 by Aliki Brandenberg. *Yawn*: By Susan Whelehan. Reprinted by permission of the author. *Sleepy People*: By M.B. Goffstein. Reprinted by permission of Farrar, Straus and Giroux, Inc. SLEEPY PEOPLE by M.B. Goffstein. Copyright © 1966 by M.B. Goffstein. *I Wouldn't*: (text only) from YOU READ TO ME, I'LL READ TO YOU by John Ciardi (J.B. Lippincott Co.). Copyright © 1962 by John Ciardi. Reprint by permission of Harper & Row, Publishers, Inc. *The Little Giant*: By Robert Kraus. Copyright © 1967 Robert Kraus. Permission granted by Robert Kraus. *My Sunday Socks*: By permission of Oak Tree Publications, Inc. Copyright © 1978 by Dr. Fitzhugh Dodson. From I WISH I HAD A COMPUTER THAT MAKES WAFFLES...by Dr. Fitzhugh Dodson. All rights reserved. *The Rain Puddle*: Entire book, without illustrations, THE RAIN PUDDLE by Adelaide Holl. Copyright © 1965 by Lothrop, Lee & Shepard Co., Inc. (A Division of William Morrow & Company). By permission of the publishers. *Sun Grumble*: By Claudia Fregosi. Reprinted with permission of Atheneum Publisher. *Where Can Red-Winged Blackbirds Live?*: By Herbert H. Wong & Matthew F. Vessell. Adapted from WHERE CAN RED-WINGED BLACKBIRDS LIVE? © 1970, by Herbert H. Wong and Matthew F. Vessel, by permission of Addison-Wesley Publishing Company, Inc. *Is Anyone Here?*: By Tammy Brooks. Reprinted by agreement with Annick Press Ltd./Books By Kids. *Teeny Tiny Ghost*: By Lilian Moore, in SEE MY LOVELY POISON IVY. Copyright © 1975 Lilian Moore. Reprinted with the permission of Atheneum Publisher. *Hester*: By Byron Barton. Entire text and six illustrations from HESTER written and illustrated by Byron Barton. Copyright © 1975 by Byron Barton. By permission of Greenwillow Books (A Division of William Morrow & Company). *October*: From SUNFLAKES AND SNOWSHINE by Fran Newman and Claudette Boulanger. Reprinted by permission of Scholastic-TAB PUblications. *Breakfast Is*: From THE SURPRISE SANDWICH—POEMS FOR CHILDREN. Reprinted by permission of Black Moss Press. *Munch Lunch*: Excerpted from the book MAKE A CIRCLE KEEP US IN: Poems for a Good Day by Arnold Adoff and illustrated by Ronald Himler. Text Copyright © 1975 by Arnold Adoff. Illustrations Copyright © 1975 by Ronald Himler. Reprinted by permission of DELACORTE PRESS and the Author. *The Tooth*: From GEORGE AND MARTHA by James Marshall. Copyright © 1972 by James Marshall. Reprinted by permission of Houghton Mifflin Company. *Snake*: By Lilian Moore from LITTLE RACCOON AND POEMS FROM THE WOODS. Copyright © 1975 Lilian Moore. Reprinted with permission of McGraw-Hill Book Company and Marian Reiner for the author. *Q Is for Duck*: By Mary Elting and Michael Folsom from Q IS FOR DUCK: AN ALPHABET GUESSING GAME by Mary Elting and Michael Folsom. Text Copyright © 1980 by Mary Elting and Michael Folsom. Pictures copyright © 1980 by Jack Kent. Reprinted by permission of Ticknor & Fields/Clarion Books, Houghton Mifflin Company. *In Kamloops*: By Dennis Lee. © Copyright, 1974, by Dennis Lee. From ALLIGATOR PIE by Dennis Lee. Reprinted by permission of Macmillan of Canada (A Division of Gage Publishing Limited). *Benjamin & Tulip*: From BENJAMIN & TULIP by Rosemary Wells. Copyright © 1973 by Rosemary Wells. Reprinted by permission of THE DIAL PRESS. *No Elephants Allowed*: From NO ELEPHANTS ALLOWED by Deborah Robison. Copyright © 1981 by Deborah Robison. Reprinted by permission of Ticknor & Fields/Clarion Books, a Houghton Mifflin Company. *If I Could Only Take Home a Snowflake*: From I DIN DO NUTTIN by John Agard is reproduced by permission of The Bodley Head. *Chicken Forgets*: From CHICKEN FORGETS by Miska Miles, illustrated by Jim Arnosky. Text © 1976 by Miska Miles. By permission of Little, Brown and Company in association with the Atlantic Monthly Press. *The Spaceship Earth*: Text adapted from PEOPLE by Peter Spier. Copyright © 1980 by Peter Spier. Reprinted by permission of Doubleday & Company, Inc. *The Surprise Party*: Reprinted with permission of Macmillan Publishing Co., Inc. from THE SURPRISE PARTY by Pat Hutchins. Copyright © 1969 by Pat Hutchins. *Hurray*: By permission of Oak Tree Publications, Inc. Copyright © 1978 by Dr. Fitzhugh Dodson. From I WISH I HAD A COMPUTER THAT MAKES WAFFLES...by Dr. Fitzhugh Dodson. All rights reserved. *Uncle Elephant Trumphets the Dawn*: (pp. 25-31) in UNCLE ELEPHANT by Arnold Lobel. Copyright © 1981 by Arnold Lobel. By permission of Harper & Row, Publishers, Inc. *Mog's Christmas*: By Judith Kerr, published Collins, © Judith Kerr 1976. *Galoshes*: From STORIES TO BEGIN ON by Rhoda W. Bacmeister. Copyright, 1940, by E.P. Dutton & Co., Inc. Renewal copyright, 1968, by Rhoda W. Bacmeister. Reprinted by permission of the publisher, E.P. Dutton. *The Guest*: Text and art of "The Guest" from OWL AT HOME, written and illustrated by Arnold Lobel. Copyright © 1975 by Arnold Lobel. An I CAN READ Book. By permission of Harper & Row, Publishers, Inc. *Where Does the Butterfly Go When It Rains?*: Reprinted from WHERE DOES THE BUTTERFLY GO WHEN IT RAINS? © 1961, by May Garelick. A Young Scott Book. By permission of Addison-Wesley Publishing Company, Inc. *The Snowy Day*: Text and selected illustrations from THE SNOWY DAY by Ezra Jack Keats. Copyright © 1962 by Ezra Jack Keats. Excerpted by permission of Viking Penguin Inc. *Windy Tree*: By Aileen Fisher from IN THE WOODS, IN THE MEADOW, IN THE SKY, Scribners, New York, 1965. Reprinted by permission of the author. *Down the Hill*: Text and art of "Down the Hill" from FROG AND TOAD ALL YEAR, written and illustrated by Arnold Lobel. Copyright © 1976 by Arnold Lobel. An I CAN READ Book. By permission of Harper & Row, Publishers, Inc. *It Was a Dark and Stormy Night*: Reprinted by permission of Four Winds Press, a division of Scholastic Inc. from ARM & ARM by Remy Charlip. Copyright © 1969 by Remy Charlip. *Sally-Ann in the Snow*: By Petronella Breinburg, illustrated by Ossie Murray, is published by The Bodley Head. *Weather Is Full of the Nicest Sounds*: Text excerpt from I LIKE WEATHER by Aileen Fisher. Text copyright © 1963 by Aileen Fisher. By permission of Thomas Y. Crowell, Publishers.

Table of Contents

One Is Me

by
Meguido Zola

One is me.
Two is ears.
Three is A B C.
Four is arms and legs.
Five is a hand.
Six is parents and grandparents.

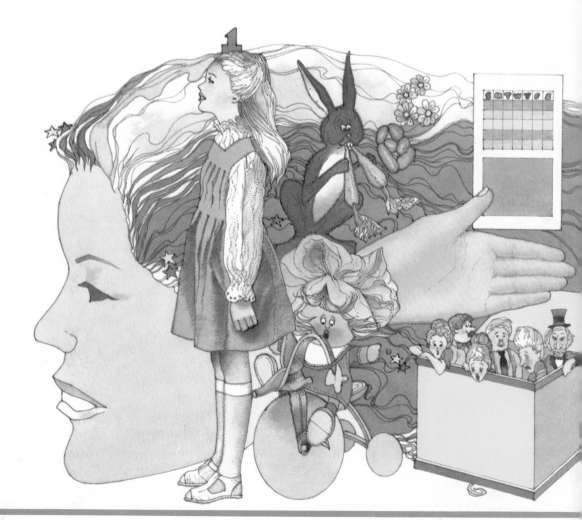

Seven is a week.
Eight is a doh ray me fah soh lah te doh.
Nine is the planets.
Ten is fingers and toes.
Eleven is my brother.
Twelve is the months of the year.
Thirteen is...I don't know.

The Animals' Walk

by
Dolores Hind

One fine day some animals left the zoo.
The animals wanted to see the city.
The animals wanted to see the buildings.
The animals wanted to see the people.
The animals wanted to see the stores.
The animals wanted to see the signs.

The elephant saw this sign.
The elephant said, "I'll sell my trunk."

The gnu saw this sign.
The gnu said, "I'll play my horn."

The lion saw this sign.
The lion said, "I'll get my hair cut."

The giraffe saw this sign.
The giraffe said, "I'll get some neckties."

The leopard saw this sign.
The leopard said, "I'll get my spots taken out."

The hippopotamus saw this sign.
The hippopotamus said, "I'll get my fat taken off."

All the animals saw this sign.
All the animals said, "We'll get some food."

Then the animals looked at the people.
The people were running in and out
of the restaurants.

The people were running in and out of the buildings.
The people were running in and out of the stores.

The people were running in and out of the cars.
The people were running in and out of the buses.

The animals said, "The city is too busy."
The animals said, "The city is too noisy."
The animals said, "The city is too crowded."
The animals said, "Let's walk back to the zoo."

And they did.

What Do I Hear?

by
David Booth

What do I hear in the mountains?
Do you hear it too?
Wind in the pines,
Water in the stream,
Eagle in the sky,
The footsteps of the grizzly as he thud-thuds by.

What do I hear in the city?
Do you hear it too?
Bells in the tower,
Children in the school,
Planes as they fly,
Tires on the roadway as the cars whiz by.

What do I hear in my house?
Do you hear it too?
Bacon in the pan,
Singing on TV,
Baby's waking cry,
Sneakers on the stairs as the children fly by.

What do I hear in the schoolroom?
Do you hear it too?
Chalk on the chalkboard,
A story being told,
Baseballs flying high,
Running on the playground as the recess speeds by.

What do I hear in my world?
Do you hear it too?

I Want
a Small Piece of String

by
Remy Charlip

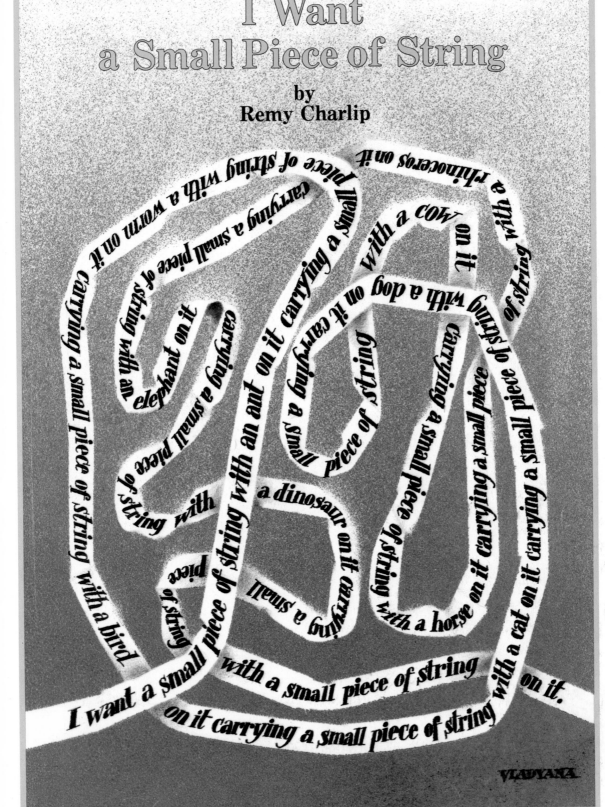

Fresh Cider and Pie

by
Franz Brandenburg

There was once a spider who caught a fly.
"I am going to eat you," she said. "Make your last wish."

"My favorite dish," said the fly, "is apple pie with a glass of cider."

"Your wish shall be granted," said the spider.

The spider fetched the apples,
baked the pie,
and pressed the cider.

"Thank you very much, Miss Spider," said the fly,
"for this good cider and pie."

"You are welcome," said the spider,
eating all of the pie
and leaving none of the cider.

"No fly has ever tasted such delicious pie," said the fly.

"Would you like a little more before you die?"
asked the spider.

"I would indeed," said the fly.

The spider baked another pie.
The fly pressed more cider.
Then the spider drank all of the cider
and left none of the pie.

"I didn't know," said the fly,
"that spiders are so good at making cider."

"Have some more!" said the spider.

"I won't say no," said the fly.

This time the spider pressed the cider
and the fly baked the pie.
For the third time the spider guzzled down the cider
and the fly watched her eat the pie.
They carried on this way
for the rest of the day.

"I don't think there is any room in me," said the spider, "for a fly full of pie and apple cider."

"It was a lovely day," said the fly. "Goodbye!"

Yawn

by
Susan Whelehan

I'm so tired.
I can't go on,
I'm so tired.
All I want to do is yawn.

I want to go right home
And fall into a heap.
I can't finish this poem
Because I'm f_all_i_ng...

Sleepy People

by
M.B. Goffstein

Sleepy people live
wherever there is room for a little bed.

There may be a family of sleepy people
living in one of your old bedroom slippers,
where they are very cozy
in their warm nightshirts and night hats.

They yawn.
Ah-ah-ah-aaaaaaaah.
They stretch.
En-en-en-eeeeeeen.
They smile.
M-m-m-mmmmmmmm.
They are always very sleepy.

Every evening the sleepy father goes to find
cocoa and cookies for a little bedtime snack.

And the children's eyes are closing
as they chew the cookies
and drink their cocoa from warm cups.

Then, while the sleepy father
snores softly,
the sleepy mother
sings to her children a little song.

"Asleep, asleep, the moon's asleep
in a soft, gray cloud.
Asleep, asleep, the bird's asleep
in his small, warm nest.
Asleep, asleep, my children sleep
in their own, good beds."

I Wouldn't

by John Ciardi

There's a mouse house
In the hall wall
With a small door
By the hall floor
Where the fat cat
Sits all day,
Sits that way
All day
Every day
Just to say,
"Come out and play"

To the nice mice
In the mouse house
In the hall wall
With the small door
By the hall floor.

And do they
Come out and play
When the fat cat
Asks them to?

Well, would you?

M. NIDENOFF 1984

The Little Giant
by
Robert Kraus

I am a giant.
I know I'm a giant,
because I have giant whiskers
and carry a giant club.
But nobody else knows it.
Grasshoppers hop at me.
Bees terrify me.
Frogs leap over me.
Flies laugh at me.
Spiders try to lure me into their webs.
And the big giant won't even say hello.

What's the good of being a giant
if you're smaller than everybody
and can't frighten anybody?

Suddenly I hear voices saying,
"Run for your life!"
"A giant! A giant!"
I look up, but I don't see a giant.
I look down, and I see two tiny ants.

"What a big, mean, ugly giant!"
says one ant.
"Not so loud—he'll hear you!"
says the other ant.
"Excuse me," I say. "Are you
by any chance talking about me?"
"Who else?" they cry,
running away as fast as they can.
"Goodbye," I say. "And thank you!"

I feel big and strong and very giant-like.
It's a wonderful feeling.
I hop at a grasshopper.
I terrify a bee.
I leap over a frog.
I laugh at a fly.
"Stay away from my web!"
pleads a spider.

Then along comes the big giant.
"Hello, giant," I say.
"Hello, giant," he says.

I know I'm a giant
and now the whole world knows it too.

My Sunday Socks

by
Dr. Fitzhugh Dodson

Monday morning I put rocks in my socks.
Tuesday morning I put my socks in a box.
Wednesday morning I put the box on a goat.
Thursday morning I put the goat in a coat.
Friday morning I put the coat in a tree.
Saturday morning I put the tree in the sea.
Sunday morning I put the socks on me!

The Rain Puddle
by
Adelaide Holl

Plump Hen was picking and pecking
in the meadow grass.
"Cluck, cluck! Cluck, cluck!"
she said softly to herself.

All at once she came to a rain puddle.
"Dear me!" she cried.
"A plump little hen has fallen into the water!"
And away she ran calling,
"*Awk, awk! Cut-a-cut! Cut-a-cut! Cut-a-cut!*"

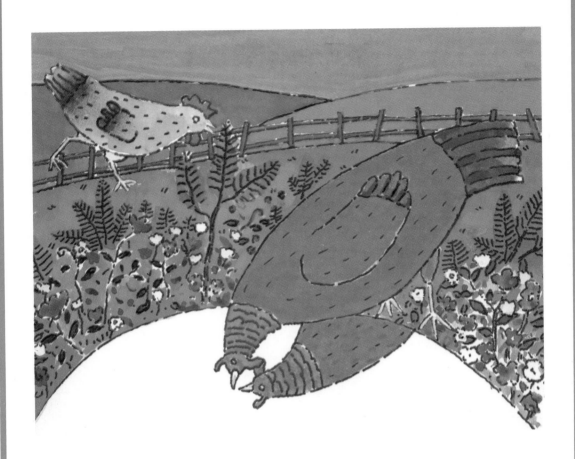

Turkey was eating corn in the barnyard.
"Come at once!" called Plump Hen.
"A hen is in the rain puddle!"
Away went Turkey to see for himself.
"*Gobble-obble-obble!*" he cried when he looked in.
"It is not a plump hen.
It is a big, bright turkey gobbler!"

Pig was crunching red apples in the orchard.
He heard the news.
Off he waddled to take a look.
"*Snort, snort! Oink, oink!*
They are both wrong," Pig said to himself.
"It is a beautiful, fat pig
that has fallen into the rain puddle.
I must get help at once!"

Curly Sheep was nibbling sweet clover in the pasture,
and Cow was softly chewing her cud
under a shady tree.
"What is going on?" they said to one another.
"Let us go and see."

They found all the other animals
crowded around the puddle together.
"A whole barnyard full of animals
has fallen into the water," they all exclaimed.
"We must run for help!"

While all the animals were running about
in great excitement, the sun came out.
The sun shone warm and bright.
It dried the rain puddle all up.

Plump Hen stopped running around in circles
and cried, *"Awk, awk! Cut, cut!* Look!
The animals have all climbed out safely!"
And away she went to pick and peck
in the meadow grass.

"*Gobble-obble-obble!* So they have!" agreed Turkey.
And off he went to eat corn in the barnyard.
"You are quite right," snorted Pig.
And he waddled off to crunch red apples
in the orchard.

Curly Sheep said, *"Baaaa, baaaa,"* and went back
to nibble sweet clover in the pasture.
"Moooo, moooo!" said Cow.
"All of the animals escaped!"
And off she went to find a shady tree
and to chew her cud.

Wise Old Owl looked down from a tree above and chuckled to himself.

The Butterfly Friends

by
Willa Pauli

There were once three butterflies—
an orange one, a red one, and a blue one—
who played in the sunshine,
and who danced on this flower
and on that flower.
They were so happy
that they never grew tired.
One day it started to rain
and they got wet,
so they tried to fly home.
                    The door was shut,
                    and they could not get in,
                        so they had to stay out in the rain,
                        and they got wetter and wetter.

So they flew over to the tulip and said,
"Good Tulip, open your flower a little for us
and let us hide from the rain."

"I shall be glad to take in the orange one,"
said the tulip. "He looks like me.
But I cannot take in the other two!"

"If you will not take in my friends,"
replied the orange one, "I shall stay wet,
rather than leave them."

The rain fell more and more heavily,
so they flew across to the lily, and said,
"Dear Lily, open your flower a little for us,
and let us hide from the rain."

"I shall be glad to take in the red and the blue one,"
said the lily, "but I cannot take in the orange one."

"If you cannot take in our friend,"
said the red and blue butterflies,
"then we shall have to do without your help."
And so they flew away together.

But the sun, who was hiding behind a cloud,
had overheard them, and it was glad
that the three butterflies loved each other.
It chased the clouds and the rain away
and dried the butterflies' wings.
So the orange, the red, and the blue butterflies
danced and played among the flowers
for the rest of the day.

Sun Grumble

by
Claudia Fregosi

One day the sun woke up
crabby and mean.
"I'm tired of shining.
I quit!" he grumbled.
So he played checkers with a star
and he cheated.

Meanwhile, it was cold and dark on earth.
"What will we do?" said the people.
"What will we do?" said the animals.
"What will we do?" said the plants.
But the sun didn't hear them.
He was kicking meteors into the little dipper.

The earth got colder and darker.
"What will we do?" cried the people.
"What will we do?" cried the animals.
"What will we do?" cried the plants.
But the sun didn't hear them.

He was talking to a huge star.
The star was shining on many small planets.
"What are you doing?" asked the sun.
"The planets need me and I'm helping them,"
replied the star.
"I'm not helping anyone!" huffed the sun.
And off he went.

The next day he decided to visit the earth.
He didn't want anyone to know who he was,
so he went in disguise.
He wrapped his sunbeams in a cloud,
and sneaked down to earth.

There were no birds
singing in his long sunbeams.
It was cold and black.
There were no cats
sleeping in his patches of sunlight.

"Oh, where is the sun?" moaned the people.
"Oh, where is the sun?" moaned the animals.
"Oh, where is the sun?" moaned the plants.
"He's where he pleases.
He can do whatever he wants,"
snorted the sun.

And then he looked at the earth.
It was *so* cold and black.
"Harrumph," he grumbled.
"What a mess!"
And with that he threw away his disguise
and poked the clouds with his sunbeams
until the earth was warm and bright again.

The Troll Bridge

by
Lilian Moore

This is the Bridge
of the
Terrible Troll.
No one goes
by
without paying
a toll,
a terrible toll,
to the Troll.

It's no place to
loll, to
linger or
stroll,
to sing or to
play.
So if ever you
ride
to the
opposite side,
be ready to
pay
the terrible troll—
I mean, terrible toll—
to the Terrible Toll—
I mean, Troll.

Where Can Red-Winged Blackbirds Live?

by
Herbert Wong and Matthew Vessel

Birds!
Look at all of them!

Some have red on the wings.
They are red-winged blackbirds.
There are other birds, too.
Where are they all going?

The birds fly over the city.
Will they stop?
Some birds live in the city.
This flock of birds will not find food here.
They cannot make homes here.
The birds fly on.

Now they are over a desert.
The birds come down.
There is just a little water here.
The desert habitat is dry.
The birds are ready to fly away.
Are all of them going?
No. Some birds will stay.
These are orioles that live in the desert.
The orioles can live in a dry habitat.
But the red-winged blackbirds
and the others are going.
They cannot live in the desert
with the orioles.

How black this forest is!
At one time it was green.
There were many animals here then.
Now there is very little food.
Not many of the animals are here now.
This forest is not a good habitat for them.
The flock of birds will not stop.

This forest is green.
A deer looks up.
And two little deer!
The birds are coming down.
They can find food and water here.
They can stay here for a time.

The birds fly over what was once a meadow.
The meadow is people habitat now.
Airplanes fly in and out.
Cars and trucks come and go.
Many people work here.
The birds fly on.

Kong-ka-ree, kong-ka-ree!
What makes that noise?
Is it a bird?
It is in the cattails.
It calls again. *Kong-ka-ree!*
There are red-winged blackbirds in the cattails!

The flock of red-winged blackbirds flies to the cattails.
This pond is a good habitat for the birds.
They had to fly a long way to find it.
But now they will make their homes here.
Kong-ka-ree!

Two Halloween Stories

by
David Booth

Story Number One

Pamela loved Halloween.
She made her costume in September.
She tried it on every night to make sure that it still fit.
Pamela loved to eat.
That is the reason why Pamela loved Halloween.
She wanted to collect all of the treats.

This year Pamela was going to dress up like a gypsy.
She made a gypsy skirt, a gypsy hat,
and she bought shiny, gold gypsy earrings.
When Pamela tried on her costume,
she looked just like a gypsy.
Pamela decided to collect her treats in a knapsack.
She knew that gypsies traveled around the country.
Pamela was going to travel around the block.

On Friday night at 6:00 p.m., Pamela ate a big supper, then she set out for her trick-or-treat trip.
She knocked at the neighbor's door.
No one was home.
Pamela felt nervous.
She looked at her gypsy costume.

She looked like a gypsy all right.
She knocked at number 26 Oak Street.
No one was home.
She knocked at number 28, number 30,
number 32, number 34, and number 36 Oak Street.
No one was home.
Pamela felt sad.
She decided to go home.

Just then the bus stopped at her corner.
Pamela saw her neighbors getting off the bus.
"Hello, Pamela," said Edward.
"Why are you dressed up like a gypsy?"
Pamela said, "It's Halloween,
and I am going trick or treating."
"Oh, Pamela," said Edward, "tomorrow is Halloween.
I have just bought my treats
for you and the other children."

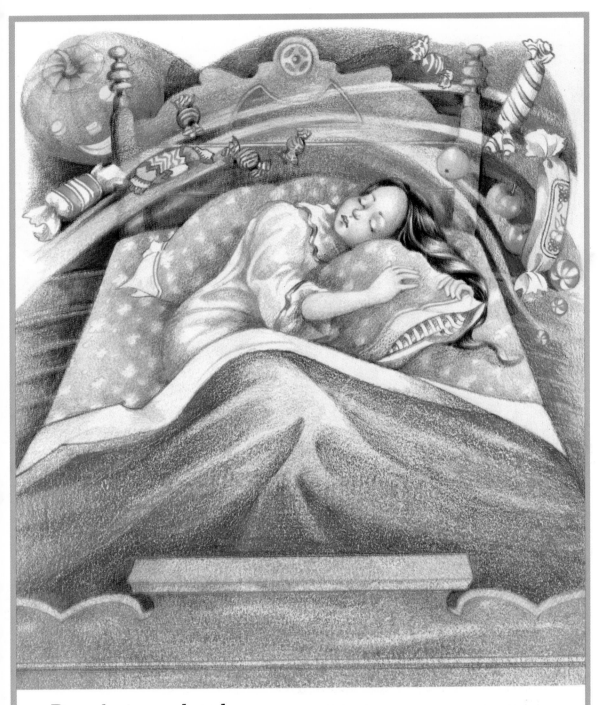

Pamela turned red.
She said goodnight and went home.
She ate another helping of dessert.
Then she took off her gypsy costume
and put on her pajamas.
She went to sleep and dreamed of tomorrow's treats.

Story Number Two

Come to
a Hallowe'en Party
at Miguel's House
October 31, 7:00-8:30 p.m.
P.S. Wear a costume
and mask.

Miguel was having a Halloween Party.
He invited all of his friends.
The invitation looked like a pumpkin.

Miguel and his parents decided to have hot dogs,
apple juice, and a cake shaped like a pumpkin.
Miguel decided to dress up like a clown.
He had a clown costume that he wore last year.
Halloween night, Miguel found his costume.
He tried it on.
It did not fit.

Miguel had grown too much
to wear his clown costume!
What would he wear to the party?
Suddenly, Miguel's father had an idea.
He found a large box and cut a hole for the head,
two holes for arms, and two more for legs.

Then he painted the box silver.
Miguel's mother put silver make-up on Miguel's face.
Miguel practiced walking and talking like a robot.
That night, everyone came to the party.
There were clowns, witches, ghosts,
gypsies, vampires, and cowboys.

But there was only one robot!

Is Anyone Here?

by
Tammy Brooks

Is anyone here?
A bird,
a mouse,
a cat,
or dog?
Is anyone here?
A boy,
a girl?
Is there anyone here
to play with
or to talk to?
I am alone in the woods all by myself.
Is anyone here?
Is anyone here?

The Teeny Tiny Woman

A Folktale
Retold by Jo Phenix

Once upon a time
there was
a teeny tiny woman
who lived in
a teeny tiny house.

One day
the teeny tiny woman
put on
her teeny tiny bonnet
and went out of
her teeny tiny house
to take
a teeny tiny walk.

The teeny tiny woman
had only gone
a teeny tiny way
when she came to
a teeny tiny gate.

The teeny tiny woman
opened
the teeny tiny gate
and went into
a teeny tiny garden.

Now in this
teeny tiny garden
the teeny tiny woman
began to pick
some teeny tiny beans.
She put them in her
teeny tiny basket.
Then the teeny tiny woman found
a teeny tiny bone.

The teeny tiny woman
put the teeny tiny bone
into her teeny tiny pocket
and ran home.

Then the teeny tiny woman
put the teeny tiny bone
in her teeny tiny cupboard.

She was a teeny tiny bit tired,
so she climbed
the teeny tiny stairs
and got into
her teeny tiny bed.

The teeny tiny woman
had slept
a teeny tiny time
when she was awakened.
A voice was saying:

The teeny tiny woman
hid her teeny tiny head
deeper under her teeny tiny covers,
but the voice spoke again:

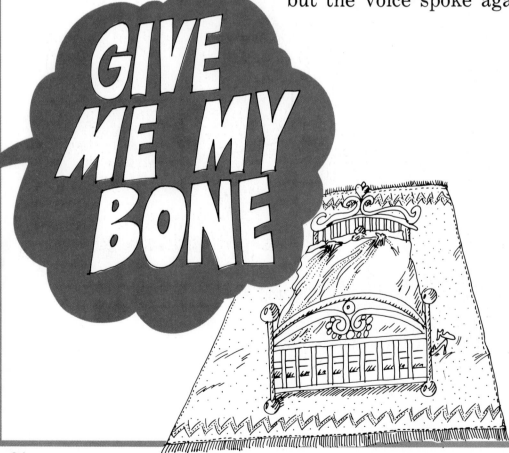

The teeny tiny woman
hid her teeny tiny head
under her teeny tiny covers,
but the voice spoke again:

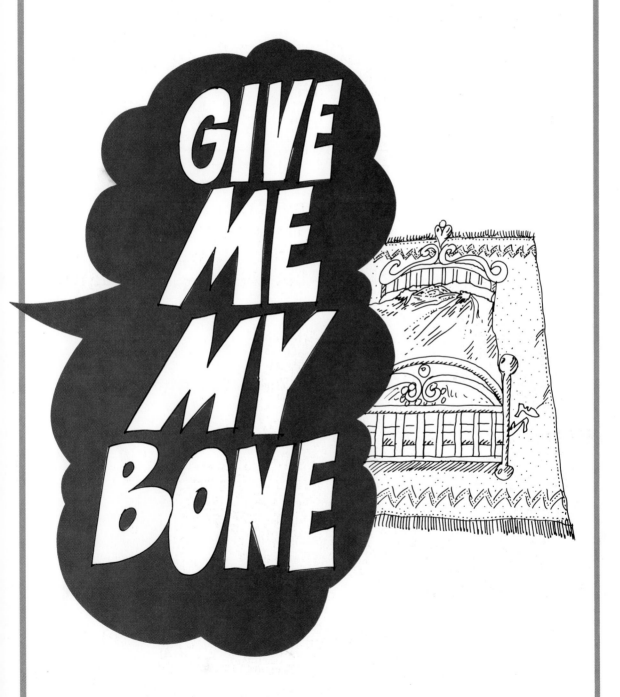

GIVE ME MY BONE

Then
the teeny tiny woman
poked her teeny tiny head
out from under the covers,
and said:

Teeny Tiny Ghost

by
Lilian Moore

A teeny tiny ghost,
no bigger than a mouse,
at most,
lived in a great big house.

It's hard to haunt
a great big house
when you're
a teeny tiny ghost,
no bigger than a mouse,
at most.

He did
what he could do.

So, every dark
and stormy night—
the kind that shakes
a house with fright—
if you stood still
and listened right,
you'd hear a
teeny
tiny
BOO!

Hester

by
Byron Barton

Hester was dressed early for her Halloween party.
While she waited for her friends to arrive,
she decided to go out to all of her neighbors
for trick-or-treats.
But she soon decided that she would look
for a more unusual place to spook.

I'll try this house, Hester thought.
She went up to the door and rang the bell.
An old lady answered and Hester yelled,
"TRICK-OR-TREAT!"

The lady smiled.
"Come in, my dear."
"These are my friends,"
the lady said.
"Won't you join us?"

Hester was polite.
"Hello," she said.

"This is a very nice house you live in."

"Thank you," said the old lady. "You're very kind.
Would you like to see more?"

The lady showed Hester the rest of the house.
"This is my favorite room," she said.
"And these are my favorite clothes
and my favorite hat and my favorite broom."

"Would you like to go for a ride?"
With the old lady up front and Hester behind,
they went flying into the night.
High above the buildings, the two of them flew.
Then they came back,
but a little too fast and CRASH!!

The broom was broken into bits.
"Here, take mine," Hester said.

"Thank you, my dear," said the old lady.
Then Hester said goodbye and hoped
she would see them all again next year.

Hester hurried home to her party.
When Hester got home, her mother wondered
what happened to her broom.
But before Hester could explain,
her friends began to arrive.
And they all had a wonderful time.

October

by
Fran Newman and Claudette Boulanger

Sally, hi! I'm glad you came.
Boy, you sure don't look the same!

Sally, gee, I like your hat.
You look weird dressed up like that.

Sally, who'd believe the change?
Your face and hands are really strange.

Sally, that's a scary wig!
How'd you make your eyes so big?

Sally, wait! What did you say?

Sally?...

Gosh, she flew away!

Breakfast Is

by
Red Lane

My favorite breakfast
is a fried egg sandwich.

My father's favorite breakfast
is ham and eggs.

My mother's favorite breakfast
is toast and jam.

My brother's favorite breakfast
is cereal flakes with brown sugar on.

My dog's favorite breakfast
is porridge.

One morning there were
no eggs for breakfast
and there was no ham
and no bread for toast
and no jam
and no cereal flakes
and no brown sugar.

So,
my mother got out some oatmeal
and made some porridge
and we all ate porridge for breakfast,
just like my dog's porridge.

And my dog ate the most.
And when we'd finished,
my father got up from the table
and said, *"Bow wow."*

And we all laughed
and my dog jumped up and down
and I think he was laughing, too.

What do you think?

Munch Lunch

by
Arnold Adoff

munch
lunch
  at
noon
  peanut
  butter
in a
spoon
  some
  soup,
more
milk
ma ma
  makes
munch
lunch

The Tooth

by
James Marshall

One day, when George was skating to Martha's house,
he tripped and fell. And he broke off
his right front tooth. His favorite tooth, too.

When he got to Martha's, George cried his eyes out.
"Oh dear me!" he cried. "I look so funny
without my favorite tooth!"

"There, there," said Martha.

The next day George went to the dentist.
The dentist replaced George's missing tooth
with a lovely gold one.

When Martha saw George's lovely new golden tooth,
she was very happy.
"George!" she exclaimed. "You look so handsome
and distinguished with your new tooth!"

And George was happy, too.
"That's what friends are for," he said.
"They always look on the bright side and
they always know how to cheer you up."

"But they also tell you the truth,"
said Martha with a smile.

Snake

by
Lilian Moore

Snake
slides,
Snake
slithers,
like wind over
grass.

Safe in this tree,
I
watch him
pass.

Q Is for Duck

by
Mary Elting and Michael Folsom

 is for Zoo

Why?

Because Animals live in the Zoo

 is for Dog

Why?

Because a Dog Barks

C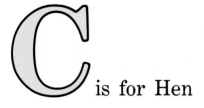 is for Hen

Why?

Because a Hen Clucks

D is for Mole

Why?

Because a Mole Digs

 is for Whale

Why?

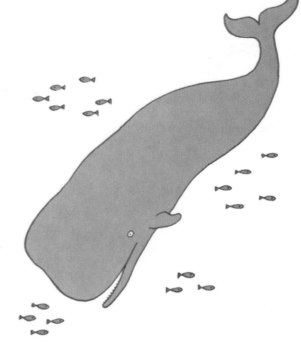

Because a Whale is Enormous

 is for Bird

Why?

Because a Bird Flies

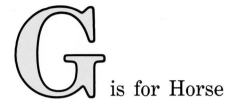 **G** is for Horse

Why?

Because a Horse Gallops

H is for Owl

Why?

Because an Owl Hoots

I

is for Mosquito

Why?

Because Mosquito bites Itch

J

is for Kangaroo

Why?

Because a Kangaroo Jumps

 is for Mule

Why?

Because a Mule Kicks

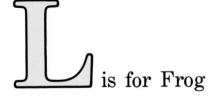 is for Frog

Why?

Because a Frog Leaps

M is for Cow

Why?

Because a Cow Moos

N is for Cat

Why?

Because a Cat Naps

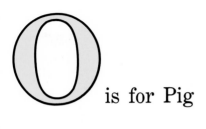 is for Pig

Why?

Because a Pig Oinks

P is for Chick

Why?

Because a Chick Peeps

Q is for Duck

Why?

Because a Duck Quacks

R is for Lion

Why?

Because a Lion Roars

S is for Camel

Why?

Because a Camel Spits

T is for Elephant

Why?

Because an Elephant Trumpets

U

is for Prairie Dog

Why?

Because Prairie Dogs live Underground

V

is for Chameleon

Why?

Because Chameleons seem to Vanish

 is for Snake

Why?

Because a Snake **W**iggles

 is for Dinosaur

Why?

Because Dinosaurs are e**X**tinct

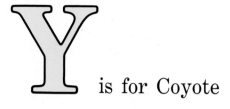 **Y** is for Coyote

Why?

Because a Coyote Yowls

 **Z** is for Animals

Why?

Because

Animals live in the Zoo

In Kamloops

by
Dennis Lee

In Kamloops
I'll eat your boots.

In the Gatineaus
I'll eat your toes.

In Napanee
I'll eat your knee.

In Winnipeg
I'll eat your leg.

In Charlottetown
I'll eat your gown.

In Crysler's Farm
I'll eat your arm.

In Aklavik
I'll eat your neck.

In Red Deer
I'll eat your ear.

In Trois Rivières
I'll eat your hair.

In Kitimat
I'll eat your hat.

And I'll eat your nose
And I'll eat your toes
In Medicine Hat and Moose Jaw.

Benjamin and Tulip

by
Rosemary Wells

Every time Benjamin passed Tulip's house she said, "I'm gonna beat you up."

1

And she did.

2

3

"Looks like he's been in a fight with Tulip again, and it looks like he got the worst of it," said sister Natalie.

"That sweet little girl," said Aunt Fern.

4

Benjamin was cleaned up
and sent to the store.

5

But first he had to go
past Tulip's house.
"This is my brand new suit,"
said Benjamin.

6

"I'm gonna mess it up!"
said Tulip.

7

And she did.

8

9

Benjamin went on to the grocery store
in a daze.

10

"One watermelon, please,"
said Benjamin.

"How about some soap?"
asked the grocer.

11

On the way back,
Benjamin had to pass
Tulip's house.
He held the watermelon
over his head. "Maybe she won't know
who I am," he thought.

12

13

But she did.

14

15

"Where is the watermelon?"
asked Aunt Fern.

"Back a ways," said Benjamin.

16

"This time," said Aunt Fern, "come back
with the watermelon and without bothering
that sweet little Tulip, or you can forget
about dinner tonight."

17

Benjamin went back to fetch his melon.
When he saw Tulip,
he zipped up the nearest tree.

18

"You're cruising for a bruising!" said Tulip.

"I've got all night," Benjamin sighed.
"I won't get dinner now anyway."

19

"I'm coming to get you!"
Tulip growled.

20

21

22

23

"Get out of that melon and let me up!" said Tulip.

"I can't hear you," said Benjamin.

24

"I'll give you three to get out of that melon!"
Tulip shrieked.

"Wait till I get out of this melon," said Benjamin.

25

"There!"

26

27

28

No Elephants Allowed

by
Deborah Robison

Justin knew that every night
after he got into bed
an elephant came into his room.

Everyone said it wasn't true.

"It's impossible, Justin," said his sister.
"There's no elephant near here."

"Don't worry, Justin," his father said.
"An elephant can't come in our house."

"It isn't real, Justin," said his mother.
"It's only a dream."

But Justin knew that every night
an elephant came into his room.

And not only one.

Sometimes two.

One day Justin's father came home
with a present for Justin.
It was a toy rabbit.
"This rabbit will help you
with those elephant problems," said Justin's father.
"He will sleep next to you
and be your friend."

The rabbit was soft and fuzzy,
and Justin liked to hold him at night.

But the rabbit didn't keep the elephants away.

"I have a good idea," said Justin's mother.
"Let's build you a new bed.
A place just for you.
No elephants allowed."
So Justin and his mother sawed
and hammered and painted—
and they made Justin a new bed.

It was a cozy bed
and a strong one.
Justin liked to sleep there
with his rabbit.

But the bed didn't keep the elephants away.

It didn't keep the lions away, either.

"Look Justin," his sister said.
"This is a special light for you.
I'll put it in your room
and you can turn it on yourself.
Now you can SEE that there are no elephants
or lions here."

Justin liked his new light.
When he was in bed with his rabbit
the light could make the darkness disappear
from the corners of his room.

But the elephants and the lions were still there.
And they brought the alligators with them.

Just before bedtime one night,
Justin was sitting in the living room
looking at magazines.
The magazines were full of pictures
and Justin loved pictures.

He turned one page and then another page.
And then he saw a picture
that made him smile.

"Mother," he said. "I need the scissors.
I want to cut out a picture
to hang up in my room."

"How nice," said his mother.
"A pretty picture in your room
will make you feel better at night."

Justin took the magazine and scissors
to his room and closed the door.

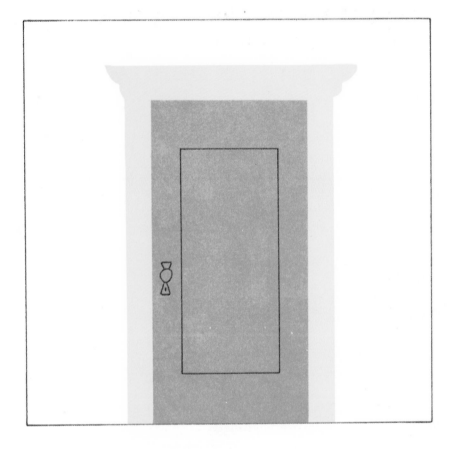

"A picture of flowers would be good,"
his father called.
"Are you cutting out flowers?"

"No," answered Justin.

"Did you find a clown?" his sister asked.
"A clown could cheer you up."

Justin giggled.
"It isn't a clown," he said.

Finally Justin opened his door.
"I'm done!" he said. "Look!
That's my picture."

"Now I have a gorilla to protect me!"

Justin climbed into bed and went to sleep.

And the elephants, the lions, and the alligators never came back again.

Winter Is on Its Way

by
David Booth

Winter is on the Way

How do you prepare for winter?
Trees and shrubs,
people and pets,
creatures big and small,
all must get ready
for the new season,
the season of wind and snow,
of frozen puddles
and leafless trees.
Our noses and toes
tell us
that Old Man Winter
will arrive
before we know it.

Story 1: The Geese Arrive

It is autumn.
The grass is brown and tired
after the summer.
Frost has colored the leaves on the trees.
Each year,
my family goes to watch the geese
getting ready to fly south.
We drive out to the pond
six kilometers from the city.
We drive over the bridge.
We leave the car
and walk to the edge of the pond.
There are no geese there.
The water is still.

We wait and listen for them to arrive.
Suddenly, we see them,
far away in the sky.
There are so many geese,
we cannot count them all.
They fly over us
as they land on the pond.
The noise of their wings flapping
is the loudest thing we have ever heard.
It is louder than an airplane.
The geese have a thousand conversations
on the pond,
about their trip, about their families,
about the dangers of the long trip.

Suddenly, the beating of their wings
fills the air again.
The geese are on their way south,
running from the winter.
They have the wind beneath their wings.
They fly in a V shape out of sight.
I take a picture of them in the sky
with my camera.
My family waves goodbye
and hurries home.
It is autumn.
The geese are gone.

Story 2: Let It Snow

When I came home from school today,
I smelled dill pickles and sweet relish.
My family is getting ready for winter.
There are over fifty jars
of wonderful things stored
in the basement, ready for winter—
pears with lemons, raspberry jelly,
peaches with cinnamon, purple and green plums,
spicy ketchup, chili sauce,
and tiny, white onions.
My family does not eat these special things
until the snow falls, until the wind howls,
until the house creaks and groans with the cold.

My family is knitting clothes
to keep us warm in winter.
My father is making a scarf for skating—
an orange and black scarf.
My mother is making warm mittens
for pulling the toboggan—
green and blue mittens.
My brother is making a hat for skating—
a brown and yellow hat.
I am making an afghan to keep us all warm
when we watch TV—a red, yellow, green,
blue, purple, pink, and black afghan.
My family does not wear these special clothes
until the snow falls, until the wind howls,
until the house creaks and groans with the cold.

My grandmother says that the birds
are getting ready for winter, too.
But they don't make pickles or knit things.
The geese and ducks fly south,
where the weather is warm.
But some birds stay here.
They eat wild berries
from the trees and bushes.

Grandfather says that some animals
change the color of their fur.
The snowshoe rabbit is turning from brown to white,
so that his enemies won't see him
against the white snow.
And he will be soft
when the snow falls, when the wind howls,
when the house creaks and groans with the cold.

I am giving the squirrels peanuts.
They are storing them in our big tree.
The groundhog in our yard
will hibernate until spring.
He has already eaten many of Grandfather's plants
and vegetables.
(He forgot to ask Grandfather first!)
The animals will be getting ready
until the snow falls, until the wind howls,
until the house creaks and groans with the cold.

If I Could Only Take Home a Snowflake

by
John Agard

Snowflakes
like tiny
insects
drifting
down.

Without a hum
they come,
Without a hum
they go.

Snowflakes
like tiny
insects
drifting
down.

If only
I could take
one
home with me
to show
my friends
in the sun,
just for fun,
just for fun.

hunt for wild blackberries

Chicken Forgets

by
Miska Miles

"Chicken," the mother hen said, "I need your help.
I want you to go berry hunting.
I need a basket of wild blackberries."

"I'd like to go berry hunting," the little chicken said.

"Take this basket and fill it to the top,"
the mother hen said. "Sometimes you forget things.
THIS time, please, please, keep your mind on
what you are doing. Don't forget."

"I won't forget," the little chicken said.
"I'll hunt for wild blackberries."

He started across the meadow.
And because he didn't want to forget,
he said to himself over and over,
"Get wild blackberries. Get wild blackberries."
All the way to the narrow river he kept saying,
"Get wild blackberries."

Then the chicken heard the rusty voice of an old frog. "What are you saying?" the frog asked.

"Get wild blackberries," the chicken said.

"If you're talking to me, you shouldn't say that," the frog said.

"Oh?" said the chicken. "What SHOULD I say?"

"Get a big, green fly," the frog said.

The chicken went on his way.
And because he didn't want to forget,
he said to himself, "Get a big, green fly.
Get a big, green fly."
All the way to the pasture he said,
"Get a big, green fly."

At the pasture, a goat pushed his head
through the rails of the fence and twitched his beard.
"If you are talking to ME," he said,
"you should NOT say, 'Get a green fly.'
You should say, 'Get green weeds.'"

"Oh?" said the chicken. And on he went,
past the pasture, saying, "Get green weeds.
Get green weeds."

A bee buzzed over his head.
"What are you mumbling?" the bee asked.

"I was only saying, 'Get weeds,'" the chicken said.

"I think that's wrong," the bee said.
"You should say, 'Get clover blossoms.'"

So the little chicken said, "Get clover blossoms."
He said, "Get clover blossoms" all the way
to the edge of the cornfield.

"No, no," said a robin. "Berries are better.
Follow me."

So the little chicken ran along the ground,
following the robin's shadow, and he came
to a beautiful patch of wild blackberries.

The robin flew down and ate
until he could eat no more.

And the little chicken filled his basket
with beautiful, shining, wild blackberries.

He started home. Back he went, through the cornfield
and beside the pasture fence by the river.
He ate five berries. Across the meadow he went.
And he ate three berries.

At home, the mother hen looked at the basket.
"You DIDN'T forget," she said. "You brought home
blackberries, and the basket is almost full."

The little chicken said, "It's easy to remember
when you really try."

"I'm proud of you," his mother said.

And the little chicken was proud, too.

The Spaceship Earth

by
Jack Booth

There are over 4 000 000 000 human beings on earth.
Every hour there are 4000 more. If we all joined hands,
the line would stretch around the world 153 times.

No two people are alike. Every one of us
is different from all the others.

We come in all sizes and shapes:
tall, short, and in between.

But everyone began very small.

We come in many colors.

Our noses come in many shapes.

So do faces, lips, and ears.

Hair can be snowy white or pitch black.

Some people have no hair at all.

People around our world wear different clothes.

People everywhere love to play.

We all need a roof over our heads.
But the homes we build are as different as we are.

We love to keep all sorts of pets.

The things we like to eat are not the same.

Most of us have to work for a living,
doing many different jobs.

There are 20 different main languages spoken on earth.

Imagine how dull the world would be if everybody would look, think, eat, dress, and act the same.

The Surprise Party

by
Pat Hutchins

"I'm having a party tomorrow,"
whispered Rabbit.
"It's a surprise."

"Rabbit is hoeing the parsley tomorrow,"
whispered Owl.
"It's a surprise."

"Rabbit is going to sea tomorrow,"
whispered Squirrel.
"It's a surprise."

"Rabbit is climbing a tree tomorrow,"
whispered Duck.
"It's a surprise."

"Rabbit is riding a flea tomorrow,"
whispered Mouse.
"It's a surprise."

"Rabbit is raiding the poultry tomorrow,"
whispered Fox.
"It's a surprise."

"Reading poetry?"
said Frog to himself.
"His own, I suppose. How dull."

The next day Rabbit went to see Frog.
"Come with me, Frog," he said.
"I have a surprise for you."

"No, thank you," said Frog.
"I know your poetry. It puts me to sleep."
And he hopped away.

So Rabbit went to see Fox.
"Come with me, Fox," he said.
"I have a surprise for you."

"No, thank you," said Fox.
"I don't want you raiding the poultry.
I'll get the blame."
And he ran off.

So Rabbit went to see Mouse.
"Come with me, Mouse," he said.
"I have a surprise for you."

"No, thank you," said Mouse.
"A rabbit riding a flea?
Even I am too big for that."
And Mouse scampered away.

So Rabbit went to see Duck.
"Come with me, Duck," he said.
"I have a surprise for you."

"No, thank you," said Duck.
"Mouse told me you were climbing a tree.
Really, you're too old for that sort of thing."
And Duck waddled off.

So Rabbit went to see Squirrel.
"Come with me, Squirrel," he said.
"I have a surprise for you."

"No, thank you," said Squirrel.
"I know you're going to sea,
but goodbyes make me sad."
And Squirrel ran up the tree.

So Rabbit went to see Owl.
"Owl," he said, "I don't know what you think I'm doing, but I'M HAVING A PARTY."
And this time everyone heard clearly.

"A party!" they shouted. "Why didn't you say so?"
"A party! How nice!"
And it was a nice party.
And such a surprise.

Hurray

by
Dr. Fitzhugh Dodson

Hurray for frogs
And tadpoles and guppies.
Hurray for goldfish
And kittens and puppies.

Hurray for puzzles
And riddles and jokes.
Hurray for popcorn,
Hot dogs, and Cokes.

Hurray for weekends,
Vacations, and school.
Hurray for Thanksgiving
And April Fool's.

Hurray for sailboats
And kites in the sky.
Hurray for cold milk
And hot apple pie!

Uncle Elephant
Trumpets the Dawn

by
Arnold Lobel

"VOOMAROOOM!"

It was morning.
I heard
a noise outside.
I ran to the window.
Uncle Elephant
was standing in the garden.

His ears flapped
in the breeze.
He raised his trunk.

"VOOMAROOOM!"

trumpeted Uncle Elephant.
"What are you doing?"
I asked.

"I always
welcome the dawn this way,"
said Uncle Elephant.
"Every new day
deserves a good,
loud trumpet."

"I have planted
all these flowers myself.
Come outside
and let me introduce you
to everyone,"
said Uncle Elephant.
"Roses, daisies,
daffodils and marigolds,
I want you to meet my nephew."

I bowed to the flowers.
Uncle Elephant
was pleased.

"This garden
is my favorite place
in the world,"
said Uncle Elephant.
"It is
my own kingdom."

"If this is your kingdom,"
I said,
"are you the king?"

"I suppose I am,"
said Uncle Elephant.

"If you are the king,"
I said,
"I must be the prince."

"Of course,"
said Uncle Elephant,
"you *must* be the prince!"

We made ourselves
crowns of flowers.

Uncle Elephant raised his trunk.

"VOOMAROOOM!"

I raised my trunk.

"VOOMAROOOM!"

We were the king
and the prince.
We were trumpeting the dawn.

I Can See Christmas
by David Booth

From her hotel room,
Holly could see the waves on the ocean.
She could see the people swimming in the water.
She could see the people sunbathing on the beach.
She could see people sitting under the big umbrellas
at the restaurant.
But Holly couldn't see Christmas.

For Holly, Christmas meant snow.
Pure, white snow.
Just perfect for sledding on with a new sled.
Just perfect for lying on to make snow angels.
Just perfect for making a big snowman.

But there was no snow here.
Just ocean and sand and beach and umbrellas.
And the calendar said December 24th.
Christmas Eve.
But Holly knew that even though tomorrow
would be December 25th,
she wouldn't be able to see Christmas.

Holly was born on Christmas day,
and Holly was certainly a Christmas name.
Christmas was Holly's favorite time of year.
She loved having her birthday on Christmas day.
It wasn't just the presents she enjoyed.
It was everything!

Holly loved shopping for presents, wrapping them,
and peeking at the ones meant for her.

She loved picking out the Christmas tree,
decorating it, and putting on the top branch the star
that she had made when she was four years old.

Holly loved baking special cakes and cookies,
and putting them in special boxes.
She loved singing carols beside the Christmas tree.
Holly loved Christmas.

But this year it was different.
Holly and her parents had gone away for Christmas.

"Far away from the snow," said Holly's mother.

"Far away from the busy time," said Holly's father.

"Far away from Christmas," thought Holly.

The trip to the sunny island
was to be everyone's Christmas present.

Now there would be no surprises
on Christmas morning.
There would be no presents to open.
There would be no relatives dropping
by to say Merry Christmas.
There would be no Christmas cookies
shaped like wreaths and Christmas stockings.

Holly loved her parents.
She did not tell them how she felt.
She wanted them to be happy on Christmas day.
But there was no Christmas in Holly's heart.

At the hotel, Holly had her own room with a door
that led into her parents' room.
Her mother and father came into Holly's room
to kiss her goodnight.
"Thank-you for agreeing to come here
for Christmas, Holly," said her mother.

"We will spend all day tomorrow playing
on the beach," said her father.

"Goodnight," said Holly, "and Merry Christmas."

"Merry Christmas, Holly," said her parents
as they closed the door.

"Well, it's not too bad," thought Holly.
"We can swim in the ocean
instead of sliding down a hill.
We can build sand castles instead of snowmen.
We can bury each other in the sand
instead of making snow angels."
Holly tried to smile, and finally fell asleep.
It was Christmas Eve.

The next morning, Holly opened her eyes.
The sun was shining in the window.
The air conditioner was humming.
It was Christmas morning.
It was also Holly's birthday.

Holly got out of bed
and walked slowly to the window.
She could see people swimming in the water.
She could see people sunbathing on the beach.
She could see people eating breakfast
under the big umbrellas at the restaurant.

Holly walked to the door leading
to her parents' room.
She knew there would be no surprises,
but she was going to say Merry Christmas
and give both her parents a big hug.

Holly opened the door and stared.
She saw a tiny Christmas tree in the corner
by the window.
She saw several presents all wrapped up
sitting under the tree.
She saw a big sign hanging on the wall
which said, "Happy Birthday, Holly."

"Merry Christmas!" said Holly's mother.

"And Happy Birthday!" said Holly's father.

Holly looked at her parents smiling at her,
and knew that Christmas was being together.

Holly saw Christmas all around her.

We Have to Get There

**by
David Booth and Meguido Zola**

Find an old barge, Marge.
Use a big tank, Frank.
Catch a fast sleigh, Fay.
We have to get there.
Where?

Hop on the bike, Mike.
Crawl in the van, Jan.
Get on the plane, Wayne.
We have to get there.
Where?

Take a dogsled, Fred.
Try a canoe, Sue,
Or a caboose, Bruce.
We have to get there.
Where?

Jump on a truck, Chuck.
Fly in a jet, Bet.
Even a tug, Doug.
We have to get there.
Where?

Galoshes

by
Rhoda W. Bacmeister

Susie's galoshes
Make splishes and sploshes
And slooshes and sloshes,
As Susie steps slowly
Along in the slush.

They stamp and they tramp
On the ice and concrete.
They get stuck in the muck and the mud.
But Susie likes much best to hear

The slippery slush,
As it slooshes and sloshes,
And splishes and sploshes,
All round her galoshes!

The Guest

by
Arnold Lobel

Owl was at home.

"How good it feels
to be sitting by this fire,"
said Owl.

"It is so cold
and snowy outside."

Owl was eating
buttered toast and hot pea soup
for supper.

Owl heard a loud sound
at the front door.
"Who is out there,
banging and pounding
at my door
on a night like this?"
he said.
Owl opened the door.
No one was there.
Only the snow and the wind.

Owl sat near the fire again.

There was another loud noise

at the door.

"Who can it be," said Owl,

"knocking and thumping at my door

on a night like this?"

Owl opened the door.

No one was there.

Only the snow

and the cold.

"The poor old winter

is knocking at my door,"

said Owl.

"Perhaps it wants to sit

by the fire.

Well, I will be kind

and let the winter come in."

Owl opened his door very wide.

"Come in, Winter," said Owl.

"Come in and warm yourself

for a while."

Winter came into the house.

It came in very fast.

A cold wind pushed Owl

against the wall.

Winter ran around the room.

It blew out the fire

in the fireplace.

The snow whirled up the stairs

and whooshed down the hallway.

"Winter!" cried Owl.

"You are my guest.

This is no way to behave!"

But Winter did not listen.

It made the window shades

flap and shiver.

It turned the pea soup

into hard, green ice.

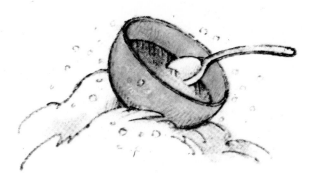

Winter went into all the rooms
of Owl's house.
Soon everything
was covered with snow.
"You must go, Winter!"
shouted Owl.
"Go away, right now!"

The wind blew

around and around.

Then Winter rushed out

and slammed the front door.

"Goodbye," called Owl,

"and do not come back!"

Owl made a new fire

in the fireplace.

The room became

warm again.

The snow melted away.

The hard, green ice

turned back

into soft pea soup.

Owl sat down in his chair

and quietly

finished his supper.

Where Does the Butterfly Go When It Rains?

**by
May Garelick**

Rain. Rain. Rain. Rain.

Where does the butterfly go
when it rains?
And the mole
and the bee
and the bird in the tree—
where do they go when it rains?

A mole can stay
in his hole.
A bee can fly back to her hive.
I've heard
that a bird
tucks its head under its wing.
But where does the butterfly go
when it rains?

I know that my cat goes scat
under the porch.
I've seen him do that when it rains.
A snake,
I suppose,
can slide between rocks.
A grasshopper can hide
in tall grass.
A rabbit can dash—
whoosh—into a bush.
But where does the butterfly go
when it rains?

I know why a duck doesn't mind the rain.
Someone told me.
A duck's feathers
are oily and slick,
so the rain doesn't stick.
Water slides off a duck's back.
Quack. Quack.

The cows I see in the field
just stand in the rain and get wet.
They eat and get wet
and eat and get wetter.
Don't cows mind the rain?

But what about minnows
and how about trout?
Where do fish go when it rains?
Pooh!
That's silly.
It doesn't rain under water.

What does a turtle do in the rain?
If I were a turtle
with a shell over me,
I would know what to do
in the rain, wouldn't you?

But what can a butterfly do?
How can it fly if its wings are wet?
Where does the butterfly go
when it rains?

And the bird in the tree
is a puzzle to me.
Even if his head is tucked
under his wing,
what happens to the rest of him,
poor thing?

As soon as the rain
stops raining so hard,
I'll go quietly
up to a tree.
And maybe I'll find
a bird in that tree,
and I'll see
what it does in the rain.

Maybe I'll find
a butterfly, too.
Then I'll know what it does
when it rains.

But where can I look?
I've never seen a butterfly
out in the rain.
Have you?

The Snowy Day

by
Ezra Jack Keats

One winter morning Peter woke up
and looked out the window.
Snow had fallen during the night.
It covered everything as far as he could see.
After breakfast he put on his snowsuit
and ran outside.
The snow was piled up very high
along the street to make a path for walking.

Crunch, crunch, crunch,
his feet sank into the snow.
He walked with his toes pointing out.
He walked with his toes pointing in.
Then he dragged his feet s-l-o-w-l-y
to make tracks.

And he found something sticking out
of the snow that made a new track.
It was a stick—a stick that was just right
for smacking a snow-covered tree.
Down fell the snow—*plop!*
—on top of Peter's head.

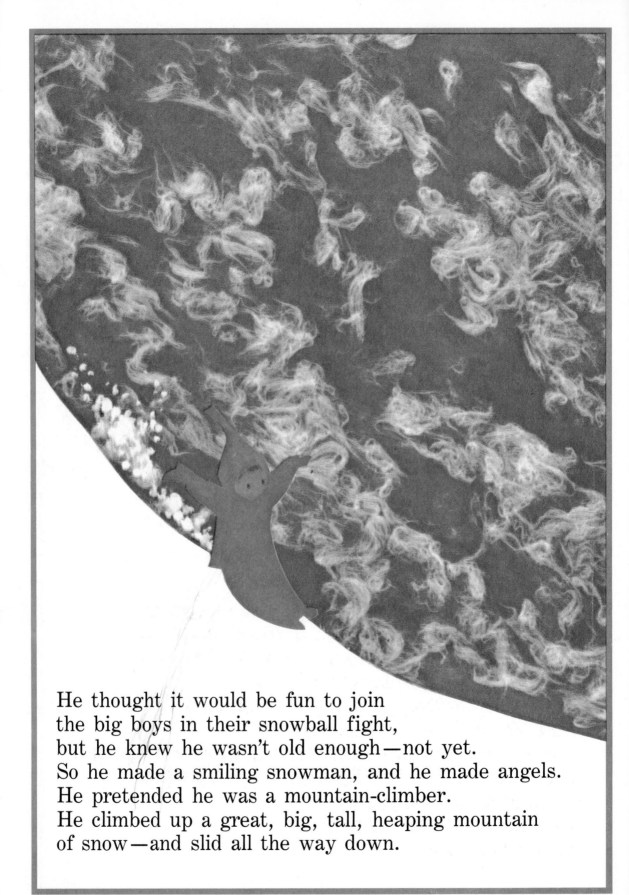

He thought it would be fun to join
the big boys in their snowball fight,
but he knew he wasn't old enough—not yet.
So he made a smiling snowman, and he made angels.
He pretended he was a mountain-climber.
He climbed up a great, big, tall, heaping mountain
of snow—and slid all the way down.

He picked up a handful of snow—and another,
and still another. He packed it round and firm,
and put the snowball in his pocket for tomorrow.
Then he went into his warm house.
He told his mother all about his adventures
while she took off his wet socks.
And he thought and thought and thought about them.
Before he got into bed he looked in his pocket.
His pocket was empty.
The snowball wasn't there.
He felt very sad.

While he slept, he dreamed that the sun
had melted all the snow away.
But when he woke up, his dream was gone.
The snow was still everywhere.

New snow was falling!

After breakfast, he called to his friend
from across the hall, and they went out together
into the deep, deep snow.

Windy Tree

by
Aileen Fisher

Think of the muscles
a tall tree grows
in its leg, in its foot,
in its wide-spread toes—
not to tip over
and fall on its nose
when a wild wind hustles
and tussles and blows.

Down the Hill

by
Arnold Lobel

Frog knocked at Toad's door.

"Toad, wake up," he cried.

"Come out and see

how wonderful the winter is!"

"I will not," said Toad.

"I am in my warm bed."

"Winter is beautiful," said Frog.

"Come out and have fun."

"Blah," said Toad.

"I do not have any winter clothes."

Frog came into the house.

"I have brought you

some things to wear," he said.

Frog pushed a coat down

over the top of Toad.

Frog pulled snowpants

up over the bottom of Toad.

He put a hat and scarf

on Toad's head.

"Help!" cried Toad.

"My best friend

is trying to kill me!"

"I am only getting you ready

for winter," said Frog.

Frog and Toad went outside.

They tramped through the snow.

"We will ride down this big hill
on my sled," said Frog.

"Not me," said Toad.

"Do not be afraid," said Frog.
"I will be with you on the sled.
It will be a fine, fast ride.
Toad, you sit in front.
I will sit right behind you."

The sled began to move
down the hill.
"Here we go!" said Frog.

There was a bump.

Frog fell off the sled.

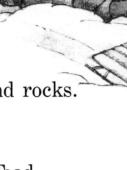

Toad rushed past trees and rocks.

"Frog, I am glad

that you are here," said Toad.

Toad leaped over a snowbank.

"I could not steer the sled

without you, Frog," he said.

"You are right. Winter is fun!"

A crow flew near by.

"Hello, Crow," shouted Toad.

"Look at Frog and me.

We can ride a sled

better than anybody

in the world!"

"But Toad," said the crow,

"You are alone on the sled."

Toad looked around.

He saw that Frog was not there.

"I AM ALL ALONE!"

screamed Toad.

Bang!

The sled hit a tree.

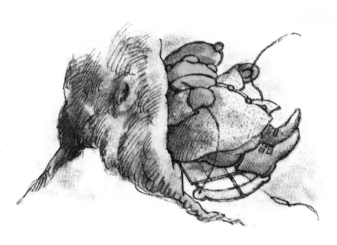

Thud!

The sled hit a rock.

Plop!

The sled dived
into the snow.

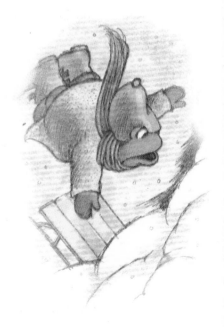

Frog came running down the hill.

He pulled Toad out of the snow.

"I saw everything," said Frog.

"You did very well

by yourself."

"I did not," said Toad.
"But there is one thing
that I can do
all by myself."

"What is that?" asked Frog.

"I can go home," said Toad.

"Winter may be beautiful,
but bed is much better."

It Was a Dark and Stormy Night

by
Remy Charlip

It was a dark and stormy night. We were standing on the deck. The ship was sinking. The captain said to me, "Tell me a story my son." And so I began, "It was a dark and stormy night. We were standing on the deck. The ship was sinking. The captain said to me, Tell me a story my son. And so I began. It was a dark and stormy night. We were standing..."

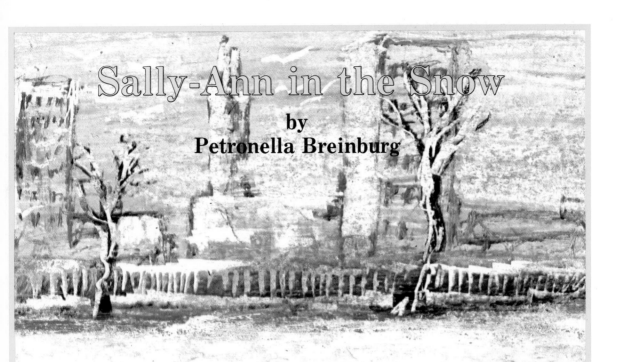

Sally-Ann in the Snow

by
Petronella Breinburg

It had snowed hard all night.
Soon all the children
would be coming out to play.

In the park, near where Sally-Ann lived,
there was a high slope.
Sally-Ann had always wanted to toboggan on it,
but she had never dared.

Sandra came to call for Sally-Ann.
"Are you coming out?" she said.
"Can I, Mum? I would love to try it," said Sally-Ann.
"Yes, you may. And your aunt will come and get you
for dinner," answered Mum.

Some children brought homemade sleighs.
Others had only a wooden box or a plank to sit on.
Everyone was joining in the fun.
Sally-Ann watched longingly.
"Have a turn in my box," offered Sandra.
"No, thank you," said Sally-Ann quietly,
not wanting anyone to see she was afraid.

A big girl had noticed, though.
"Don't try it if you're scared," she taunted.
"I know someone who knows someone else
who was scared. They made her try
                    and she broke her arm!"

Sally-Ann went over to where the younger children were playing. But they didn't want her there, either. "This part is only for the little ones."

Back on the big slope
there was a lot of laughing and shouting.
"Have a turn," someone called.
"Not if you're scared," jeered one of the boys.

"I know someone who knows someone else
who broke her leg!"
"Fibber," answered one of the girls,
throwing a well-aimed snowball.
Soon, everyone was joining in the fight.
Everyone, that is, but Sally-Ann.

She had found Sandra's box,
and, when no one was looking,
she sat in it to see how it felt.

Zoom!

Suddenly Sally-Ann was off down the slope.
She opened her mouth to let out a scream
but it was too late.
She was already at the bottom.

"I've done it! I've done it!" she shouted.

All morning Sally-Ann went up and down
the slope in Sandra's box. By the time her aunt came
to fetch her for dinner, Sally-Ann had lost count
of how many turns she had had.

One thing she was sure of, though.
"I'll never be scared of that old slope again,"
she said.

Weather Is Full of the Nicest Sounds

by
Aileen Fisher

Weather is full
of the nicest sounds:
it sings
and rustles
and pings
and pounds
and hums
and tinkles
and strums
and twangs

and whishes
and sprinkles
and splishes
and bangs
and mumbles
and grumbles
and rumbles
and flashes
and crashes.

I wonder
if thunder
frightens a bee,
a mouse in her house,
a bird in a tree?
A bear
or a hare
or a fish in the sea?

Not me!

Weather Proverbs

by
Melanie Zola

When it rains before seven:
Shine before eleven.

A sunshiny shower
Won't last half an hour.

A ring around the moon:
Rain is coming soon.

Evening red and morning gray
Will set the traveller on his way,
But evening gray and morning red
Will pour down rain upon his head.

As the days lengthen,
So the cold strengthens.

❧❧❧

The wind from the East
Is good for neither man nor beast.

March winds and April showers
Bring forth May flowers.

Whether the weather be cold,
Whether the weather be hot,
We'll weather the weather—
Whatever the weather—
Whether we like it or not!